From an **Agate** to
A Comprehensive G

Gemstone &
Crystal
Power

A Mystical
A to **Z** of stones

Robert W Wood D.Hp
(Diploma in Hypnotherapy)

Rosewood Publishing

First published in U.K. 2003
By Rosewood Publishing
P.O. Box 219, Huddersfield,
West Yorkshire HD2 2YT

www.rosewood-gifts.co.uk

Revised cover and
Re-printed in 2011

Robert W Wood D.Hp
Asserts the moral right to be identified
As the author of this work

Copy-editing
Margaret Wakefield BA (Hons) London
www.euroreportage.co.uk

Cover photograph by
Andrew Caveney BA (Hons)
www.andrewcaveneyphotography.co.uk

Cover and layout re-designed by
AJ Typesetting
www.ajtype.co.uk

Printed in Great Britain by
Delta Design & Print Ltd
www.deltaleeds.co.uk

ISBN 978-0-9567913-0-6

From an Agate to a Zircon:
A Comprehensive Guide to
Gemstone and Crystal Power

A Guide ...
. . . a book that instructs or explains the fundamentals of a subject or skill.

Gemstones and Crystals.
Suffer from headaches? Why not try a Rose Quartz. Have a bad back? Then add Hematite to your Rose Quartz. It's said that together they can work wonders on aches and pains. In physics it's well known that the energy in iron ore (Hematite) helps to boost the energy of the Quartz. If it's a very bad back then add Rock Crystal (a clear Quartz) to the combination. It acts as a catalyst to help increase the healing power and energy of the other two minerals, Rose Quartz and Hematite.

Can't sleep? No problem - put an Amethyst under your pillow, and you'll sleep like a log. Prefer to stay awake and have a bit of fun? Then add a Carnelian. Feeling a little 'naughty'? Then add Rose Quartz; it's our 'Adults Only' combination, designed for nights of passion. But do remember to watch out for that bad back.

It all sounds weird, doesn't it? 'Impossible,' I can hear you saying, 'there's no way any of this can work.' Think again. Did you know that in the medical profession there's a well-known phenomenon called a 'placebo effect'? This occurs when patients are given a dummy medicine, a sugar-coated pill. It's based on a lie, and yet many have benefited and have even been totally cured. And so just as the placebo effect has to have its sugar-coated pill, so then the crystal healer has to have a crystal.

If you thought Gemstones and Crystals were just lumps of rocks, you're in for a pleasant surprise. They are nature's little treasures, and have been around for a very long time. In fact they have been around as long as time itself, and a lot longer than any chemists.

This book has been written to help those who are interested in alternative treatments, treatments without the side-effects that drugs can have. However, common sense should tell you to see your doctor or practitioner first, before embarking on any kind of alternative treatment. The information that follows is in direct response to those that would like to know more, and is part of a series of books called 'Power for Life' - a series of books based on the mysteries surrounding gemstones and crystals; a refreshing view of an ancient wisdom. Keep an open mind and you won't go far wrong.

There are numerous ways of looking into the strange, often mystical world of gemstone and crystal powers, and you'll discover that there are many ways of explaining these mysteries too. I have spent many years researching into all the aspects of crystal power, in the search for a more modern explanation of why, once we are connected to a crystal, that crystal - or the connection - can actually be so beneficial to its user. The following information is only a 'taster' of a very large and complex subject. Before you think of dismissing all this as just hocus-pocus, think about this: at the heart of every computer are silicon chips, and what are they? They're a clear Quartz. A crystal. And crystals have power.

Believing in it.

It's often said that you have to believe in all this for it to work. But for years now, whenever I have been demonstrating crystal healing, I have always asked my audience not to believe in it, but to see what happens to them when I pass around a Rose Quartz and Hematite - a combination of stones said to work wonders on aches and pains. What better way to demonstrate and research at the same time, than with a willing audience? An audience that is just as curious as I am to see if stones do work, and if they can do what people say they can. In one year I gave over 200 talks and demonstrations, and I am no longer surprised at the number of people who tell me that they 'would never have believed it if they hadn't experienced it for themselves.' I wouldn't have known that they do work for so many, if I hadn't tried them out myself with all these audiences.

Apparently many find that their bad knees, backs, legs, necks and elbows, their headaches and their stiff joints do seem to benefit, or even be cured by this demonstration. Is it all in the mind? It's for you to decide; but remember this. In hypnosis, if you suggest to a person that the ice cube you have just placed in their hand is in fact a burning ember, once that thought strikes home then a blister will appear. On the other hand, think of a firewalker, walking on burning hot embers and not getting any blisters. 'Mind over matter' does exist.

Crystal power.

According to quantum physics, everything in the universe has an atomic structure - and that includes gemstones and crystals. They contain atomic energy, and this is the most powerful energy known on earth. Others talk of colour frequency. Red, orange and blue may seem to be different colours, but they are in fact all part of the same spectrum of light. Similarly, we tend to think of light, heat and radio waves as being different from each other, but there is a connection. The electromagnetic spectrum represents the complete range of radiation including gamma rays, X-rays, ultraviolet light, visible white light (visible to the human eye), infra-red light, microwaves and radio waves. Just because we can't see it, that doesn't mean it's not there - and it may be the same with gemstone and crystal power.

We can't hear dog whistles, but dogs can; we can't see ultraviolet light, but bees can. Just as our ears can only hear part of the range of possible sounds and cannot hear a dog whistle, so our eyes can only see a small central section of the electromagnetic spectrum of light. The power associated with Gemstones and Crystals falls into this 'can't be seen or heard' category.

Want to change your Luck?

Gemstones and Crystals have been used as lucky charms, amulets and talismans for thousands of years. Want to win the lottery? Then try a Green Aventurine - it's said to be a 'money magnet'. Or, if you play bingo, then try Obsidian Snowflake - it's a lucky talisman. Use a Tiger Eye (from South Africa) to take away your worries; or a Black Onyx to lose weight. It's the weight watchers' friend; it helps with self-control - we call it 'lose a stone'. Need to improve your memory? Then use a Rhodonite.

Within this book you'll find all the information you'll need about the metaphysical, astrological and physical properties of Gemstones, Crystals and minerals. I have scrutinised many sources and cross-referenced all the information to enable me to produce this guide. In short I have done all the work, so that you don't have to.

How to use this Guide.

The best way to use this Guide is to read the full list of Gemstones and Crystals starting on page 7, and at the same time make notes. So, if you are looking for a healing stone for a specific ailment, read the full list, find the stone or stones, and if there are a few, then you might want to narrow them down. There are various ways of narrowing down. Trust your instincts on this one. For instance, you might find, from your research, two gemstone-crystals. It may be that for you, two are ideal. You may be surprised to find that one of the stones is your Birthstone; this would then be the one for you. Or if you have a favourite colour, and if that colour is there on your list, then go with that one. No-one is really sure how all this works; only that, for many, it does. Keep an open mind - many have been pleasantly surprised.

Colour - and the Chakras.

Another useful guide when choosing crystals could be their colour. In Sanskrit there are original teachings about an energy system known as the 'Chakras'.. When seen clairvoyantly, Chakras are wheels of light and colour. There are seven of them. The first one is found at the base or root - that is, around the base of the spine. The second is the sacral or spleen, the third is the solar plexus, and the fourth is the heart. The fifth is the throat, the sixth is the brow or 'third eye', and the seventh and final one is the crown. It's said we need all these energy centres to be open so as to enjoy optimum health. Each is associated with a colour; and these colours are the seven colours of the rainbow, and are in the same running order.

Chakras cont...

Each Chakra is linked with a particular colour in the spectrum of light. The 'root' Chakra is red; the 'sacral' or 'spleen' Chakra is orange; the 'solar plexus' Chakra is yellow; the 'heart' Chakra is green; the 'throat' Chakra is blue; the 'brow' Chakra is indigo; and finally the 'crown' Chakra is violet. I know it all may sound like gobbledygook, but the human body requires light to maintain itself. For example, our bodies produce vitamin D - necessary to make our bones and teeth strong and healthy - and this is increased as a result of exposure to sunlight. Think about this: where does the vitamin D come from? One minute it's not there and the next it is. What makes the difference? Stepping out into sunlight does - so light has a power, and you can use this knowledge to your benefit when choosing the right gemstones or crystals.

Cleansing Gemstones and Crystals.

Once you have found the right crystals and stones, it's advisable to clean them. This can quite easily be done by placing them under a running tap. Some say they should be washed in salt water; the sea is ideal, but if you're not near the sea then just add some salt to water. Others believe that gemstones and crystals can attract negative energy from other people, and, again, cleansing is a way of wiping them clean.

Whichever way you decide on, make it as ritualistic as you can; that is, do the cleaning with feeling. I know of some who will bury the stones in the ground for twenty-four hours, with the intention of allowing Mother Nature to put the energy back into the crystals. Others put the stones into a glass of water and place it in the window overnight to allow the moon to shine on it. Others place the stones onto larger clusters of crystals to be energised. There's no 'right' or 'wrong' way, only 'your' way.

Connecting to a crystal.

Once you've found your healing gemstone-crystal or your lucky talisman, your lucky charm or your birthstone, you have to connect with it. Remember the story of Aladdin and his three wishes? In the story, you'll remember, the Genie in the lamp was obliged to give three wishes to whoever owned the lamp; it didn't matter to the Genie who made the wishes. So before Aladdin could get his three wishes, firstly he had to own the lamp, and secondly he had to rub the lamp.

Here's the point: do you think if, in real life, you had Aladdin's lamp, there would ever be a time when you wouldn't know where it was? It's the same with your crystal. If at any time you are asked where it is and you don't know, then you are not connected. I am always being asked, 'How do I know if I am connected?' and the easiest answer I have found over the years is this: if you lost your crystal and didn't know you'd lost it, then you were not connected. Now enjoy the journey and find your special Gemstone.

Any information given in this book is not intended to be taken as a replacement for medical advice. If in any doubt, always consult a qualified doctor or therapist.

THE MYSTICAL A TO Z OF STONES.

AGATE ... The agate probably derives its name from the small river Achates in Sicily, but can be found in many places including Brazil, Madagascar and India. Its rich variations make it a beautiful, multi-faceted stone. A powerful healer, it restores body energy and eases stressful situations; gives courage and banishes fear; calms, and increases self-esteem. A stone for good health and fortune, it helps grounding and balance. A stabiliser.

AMAZONITE ... the 'thinkers' stone'. It aids creativity and improves self-worth. A confidence stone. It attracts money and success. A soothing stone; a giver of energy. Solid blue to turquoise, it works on the throat - the fifth Chakra. It inspires hope and is sometimes also called 'the hope stone'.

AMBER ... not a stone, but the fossilised resin of extinct pine trees. Good for the throat - the fifth Chakra. Worn by actors for good luck and a clear voice. Changes negative energy into positive and is often used as a lucky talisman. It helps the body to heal itself. It is calming, lifting heaviness and allowing happiness to shine through. It prolongs life with a clear the mind.

AMETHYST ... purple to dark violet, known by a variety of names: Bishop's Stone, Stone of Healing, of Peace, of Love. St. Valentine implied it was one of the best gifts between lovers. Aids creative thinking. Relieves insomnia when placed under the pillow. A powerful aid to spiritual awareness and healing. Helps with meditation, inspiration, intuition and divine love. A stone which helps to attract that special partner.

APACHE TEARS ... a variant of Obsidian, dark, smokey, translucent in colour. Good for grounding; transforms; aids in the release of deep emotions. Eases pain, loss and sadness. Neutralises negative magic.

APATITE ... blue in colour. Strengthens muscle tissue, aids co-ordination, assists with stuttering and hypertension, and helps to fight viruses. Can help with communications, especially after a misunderstanding.

AQUAMARINE ... a Beryl, clear blue-green. It represents an ocean of love. Preserves innocence, brings spiritual vision, calms the mind and lifts the spirits, releases anxiety and fear. It is recommended for those suffering a lot of grief. Gives insight and perception in dealings with people. Gives protection, often used as a good luck charm. Leads to greater self-knowledge, quickens the mind, promotes clear and logical thinking.

AVENTURINE ... a variety of Quartz, usually green with mica inclusions. Stabilises by inspiring independence, well-being and health. Acts as a general tonic on the physical level. If left in water overnight, it can then be used to bathe the eyes, and similarly to treat skin irritations. Encourages creativity, gives courage, independence, calmness and serenity. It is a money magnet and a good luck stone, a lucky talisman.

AZURITE ... deep blue to blue-purple. An aid for meditation, it is used to increase psychic powers as it helps to induce prophetic dreams, intuition and understanding. It's also known as the 'Decision Maker'. With its high copper content it assists the flow of energy throughout the nervous system, strengthens the blood and is used to treat arthritis and joint disabilities.

BERYL ... many colours. The best of the Beryl group are emeralds and aquamarines. In ancient rituals the Beryl was used to bring rain. It is related to the sea and guards its wearer against drowning and sea-sickness. Protects against 'mind games'. Helps to stimulate the mind, and increases confidence. In the sixteenth century, it was worn to win arguments and debates.

BLOODSTONE (Heliotrope) ... a form of Jasper - dark green in colour, with red flecks. The red flecks are symbolic of Christ's death and his blood spilling onto the stone. Acts on all of the Chakras, a physical healer and a mental balancer. Removes toxins and aligns energies, especially along the spinal cord. Helps prevent miscarriages and eases childbirth. Works to overcome depression and pain of the emotional kind. Calming, grounding and revitalising. A stone to attract wealth, often used in business or legal matters to help attract success.

CALCITE ... red, orange, yellow, green and blue (see the Chakras). There is also a clear variety of calcite called Iceland Spar which, when placed over a line on a piece of paper, will produce a double image. Calcite is a strong balancing stone, giving comfort and lifting depression. Also alleviates fear, aids mental clarity, calms turbulent emotions, expands awareness and aids intuition. Good for pancreas and spleen. Clears toxins by gently helping to cleanse the blood.

CARNELIAN (Cornelian) ... mainly bright orange. The 'friendly one' - it is a very highly evolved healer. A good balancer; can help you connect with your inner self. Good for concentration. Brings joy, sociability and warmth. Good for rheumatism, arthritis, depression, neuralgia, and helps to regularise the menstrual cycle. When coupled with amethyst, purifies consciousness, reverses negative thoughts and shakes off sluggishness.

CAT'S EYE ... golden to mid-yellow, green to bluish brown. The Greeks called it 'Cymophane' meaning 'wave-light'. It resembles the contracted pupil of a cat's eye. In the symbolic necklace of 'Vishnu' the green gem was held to represent the earth. A magnetic centre of human passions. It is used to increase beauty and wealth, to protect, and to guard against danger.

CELESTITE ... white to clear; light blue cluster crystals. Signifies honesty. Helps with tiredness, soothes nerves and stress. Quietens the mind, promotes compassion, expands creative expression, reveals truth.

CHALCEDONY ... soft blue, translucent, belonging to a large group of crystalline forms and geodes. Stimulates optimism and enhances spiritual creativity. Diminishes nightmares and fear of the dark. A stone that guards travellers, and helps grounding through negative times. Banishes fear, mental illness, hysteria and depression.

CHRYSOCOLLA ... blue to blue-green opaque mineral, essentially a copper-element mineral. 'The woman's friend', relieving tension, pains and problems, soothing period pains and pre-menstrual tension. Increases energy, wisdom and peace of mind. Alleviates feelings of guilt, clears all negativity and brings about patience and contentment. Helps to attract love.

CHRYSOPRASE ... an apple-green form of chalcedony, the colour being due to traces of nickel. For wisdom and meditation. Helps the wearer to see clearly into personal problems, especially sexual frustrations and depressions. Worn to lift the emotions, attract friends and shield against negativity.

CITRINE ... clear to yellow-orange. Natural citrine was originally amethyst, transformed by being reheated and burnt in the earth's crust. Helps to clear mental and emotional problems and improve memory. Enhances willpower, optimism and confidence. Helps those who feel they have lost their way in life and need to find a new sense of direction. Strengthens the immune system, improves poor circulation and aids tissue regeneration. Placing a single crystal or cluster into a safe, till or cash box helps to attract ever-increasing financial income.

COPPER ... mixes easily with other metals; for example, copper, tin and zinc make bronze. Copper is thought to be one of the best transmitters of healing energy. This may be because it has been used very successfully against cholera; it was discovered that men who worked with copper didn't get cholera, and that wearing copper improves the metabolism, reduces inflammation and increases blood flow. Worn next to the skin it soothes arthritis and rheumatism and can kill all kinds of bacteria. Certain bacteria are found in plenty on silver coins but are said never to be found on copper.

CORAL ... red, pink or white. Calcium calcite was once a living sea creature and is therefore thought to contain 'life essence'. It is used as a protector, especially to safeguard children. Sometimes referred to as the 'Tree of Life of the Ocean', it protects and strengthens the wearer's emotional foundation. Also, because it symbolises fertility, it offers a defence against sterility.

DIAMOND ... a well-known mineral, the purest and hardest substance in nature. It forms the neatest and sharpest of all known cutting edges and is now used in microsurgery with spectacular effect. When used with loving, clear intent, it clears blockages and opens the crown Chakra. Amplifies the full spectrum of energies in the mind, body and spirit.

DIOPTASE ... deep blue to green. Rivals the Emerald in its beauty and holistic healing powers. It empowers the heart with new depth, strength, healthiness, courage, and the ability to love deeply again. Promotes genuine, sincere emotional balance, self-worth and deep well-being; helps heal sadness, heartache, abuse and neglect. A stone for the heart.

EMERALD ... green. An excellent general healer, used in ancient times as a blood detoxifier and anti-poison. Improves creativity, imagination, memory and quick-wittedness. Helps the intellect and improves intelligence. Gives power to see the future. Grants success in business ventures and offers patience, harmony, peace and prosperity. An emotional stabiliser.

FLUORITE (Fluorspar) ... appears in all rainbow colours. A 'new age' stone that strengthens thought and balances mental energy. Good for meditation. Fluorite clears the mind of stress and aids sleep. Helps physical and mental healing and strengthens bone tissue, especially tooth enamel. Relieves dental disease, viral inflammations and pneumonia.

GARNET ... black, pink-red, yellow-brown, orange or green. A member of a vast gemstone family. A 'knight in shining armour', contains a little of most metals but especially aluminium, silicon and oxygen. A revitalising tonic for the whole body, creating a shield of positive energy; aids in dreams, past lives, self-confidence and personal courage, and attracts love.

GEODES ... are hollow volcanic bubbles containing crystals. All Quartz, Rock Crystal, Amethyst and Opal is formed within geodes. The effect is brought about by the mineral-rich watery fluids percolating into the cavity or hole left by the 'bubble' which occurred in the steaming red hot volcanic lava. Some geodes are huge enough to drive cars through, while others are small enough to fit in the palm of your hand.

HEMATITE ... a natural ferric oxide, a silver-grey metallic mirror-like stone. You either like or dislike it, there's no 'in between'. To those who like it, it's a very optimistic inspirer of courage and personal magnetism. It lifts gloominess and depression and, when used in conjunction with Carnelian, can prevent fatigue. Good for blood, spleen and generally strengthens the body. Effective during pregnancy; helps with stress.

JADE ... comes in a variety of colours. It's a money magnet, a good luck talisman, and a protector from accidents, evil spirits and bad luck. It encourages long life, safe journeys, wisdom, courage, peace and harmony. The geological term for Jade is Nephrite, from the Greek word 'nephros' meaning 'kidney'. As a healer, Jade is good for kidneys, bladder, lungs and heart; the immune system, and even high blood pressure.

JASPER ... chalcedony quartz. Multi-coloured. A popular talisman, well liked amongst psychic healers. Protects from all kinds of ailments. It's a powerful healing stone, invigorating and stabilising. It calms troubled minds and helps to slow down the ageing process. Helps those suffering from emotional problems by balancing the physical and emotional needs.

JET ... a black glass-like substance - fossilised wood, another type of coal, mainly from Whitby in England. Even the Jet used in ancient Mesopotamia was thought to have been originally mined in Whitby. Like amber, when rubbed it becomes electrically charged. A good travel aid. Helps increased psychic awareness, guards against witchcraft, demons, melancholy and anxiety, and is very good for manic-depressives.

KUNZITE ... pink to dark lilac-rose. Has a high lithium content. Named after Dr G F Kunz, a noted mineralogist. Good for both the emotional and spiritual heart; reduces depression and mood swings. When held, induces relaxation by releasing tension and stress. A balancer for mind, body and spirit. Benefits those with any kind of compulsive behaviour.

KYNITE ... light blue. Contains aluminium. It is softer lengthways than it is across, and is immune to the forces of other chemicals (such as acids). Brings out our natural ability to manifest things into reality via thoughts and visualisation. Encourages devotion, truth, loyalty and reliability.

LABRADORITE ... 'irridescent Feldspar'. Yellow, pink, green, blue and violet. When in trouble and in doubt, wear a labradorite. A stone for today, it opens the energy flow to any or all of the Chakra centres, whichever is in greatest need. Brings restful sleep and straightening of the spine.

LAPIS LAZULI ... medium to dark blue with gold pyrite flecks. Called by the ancient Egyptians 'the Stone of Heaven', and thought to be the stone upon which were carved the laws given to Moses. A stone for teachers; helps ease expression and gain higher wisdom and clarity. Good for mental, physical, spiritual, psychic and emotional problems, and well-known for healing the whole. Alleviates fear and eases depression, quiets the mind; helps with creativity, writing, dreams, insight, self-expression and finding inner truth.

MALACHITE ... dark and light bands of green tints. Its name probably comes from the Greek 'malache' ('mallow', as of the colour of a green mallow leaf). Egyptians used green Malachite paste for eye make-up. Stimulates physical and psychic vision and concentration. Contains copper and is useful in treating rheumatism and arthritis. Good for raising the spirits, increasing health, hope and happiness. Brings prosperity and is used to guard against all negativity.

MOLDAVITE ... formed by a meteorite strike in the Moldau Valley area of the Czech Republic over twelve million years ago. A powerful healing stone, it helps telepathic access to spiritual laws, and attracts information from higher levels to help us and our earth to become healthier and more spiritual. Helps us to understand our true purpose in life. A stone of transformation.

MOONSTONE ... an opalescent Feldspar. In India the Moonstone is a sacred gem, thought to be lucky if given by the groom to his bride. Called the 'Travellers' Stone' because it was a favourite protective amulet for those going on perilous journeys. Claimed to promote long life and happiness. It soothes stress and anxiety and is good for period pains and other kindred disorders. A powerful fertility and good luck stone from India.

MOTHER OF PEARL ... is the lustrous, opalescent interior of various sea molluscs. Aptly dubbed the 'sea of tranquillity', it creates physical harmony of a gentle but persuasive kind. Calms the nerves. Indicates treasure, chastity, sensitivity and strength. Good for calcified joints and the digestive system. Relaxes and soothes the emotions; helps with sensitivity and stress. Carries the gentle, peaceful healing energy of the sea.

OBSIDIAN SNOWFLAKE ... not really a stone, but a volcanic glass. Also Obsidian Black, Mahogany and Clear. For all those it recognises, it's a powerful healer. Keeps energy well grounded, clears subconscious blocks and brings an insight and understanding of the power behind silence, detachment, wisdom and love. A very lucky talisman, a bringer of good fortune. Was favoured by ancient Mexican cultures to neutralise negative energy and black magic. Good for eyesight, stomach and intestines, and alleviates viral and bacterial inflammations.

ONYX ... black, 'lightweight' Quartz. It can give a sense of courage and help to discover truth. Instils calm and serenity; diminishes depression. Gives self-control whilst aiding detachment and inspiring serenity. A protective stone worn in times of conflict, a student's friend as it encourages concentration and protects against unwise decisions. It is often found in rosaries; it helps to improve devotion, and relieves stress.

OPAL ... a silica. The 'Rainbow Stone'. Multi-coloured, it is a wonderful stone to behold, and can be charged with virtually every type of energy needed. It controls temper and calms the nerves. It was sometimes considered unlucky, but (according to Thomas Nichols' book of 1652) this is probably why: 'Opalus:- cloudeth the eyes of those that stand about him who wears it, so that they can either not see or not mind what is done before them; for this cause it is asserted to be a safe patron of thieves and thefts.' Because of its beauty, things were stolen or went missing, hence, according to some, its unlucky label.

PERIDOT ... clear bright green, also green to yellow (Chrysolite). A good anti-toxin gem, for cleaning most organs and glands. An overall tonic. Used by the Egyptians, Aztecs and Incas to gently help cleanse and heal the physical, including heart, lungs, lymph and muscles. Prized by the Crusaders as 'their' stone. It clears energy pathways, strengthens the 'breath of life', and attracts prosperity, growth and openness. It's also useful for attracting love and opening new doors of opportunity and abundance.

RHODOCROSITE ... a solid to clear, beautiful pink stone. Good for giving and receiving love. Inspires forgiveness. Heals emotional scars; helps to cope with loneliness, loss, heartache, fears, insecurities and inner child issues. Helps prevent mental breakdown and balances physical and emotional traumas. Soothes and de-stresses the body, cheers the depressed and coaxes back the life force in the very sick.

RHODONITE ... pink with black inclusions. Improves memory, calms the mind and reduces stress. Gives confidence and self-esteem. Cheers the depressed, preserves youth and retards the ageing process. Helps to bring back the life force into the sick. Carries the power to the unobstructed love. Good for emotional trauma, mental breakdown, spleen, kidneys, heart and blood circulation. A very special stone.

ROCK CRYSTAL ... also known traditionally as Clear Quartz. This stone holds a place of unique importance in the world of gems. It enlarges the aura of everything near to it, by acting as a catalyst to increase the healing powers of other minerals. Its vibration resonates with the beat of life, giving Rock Crystal a key role in all holistic practices. Good for the mind and soul, strengthening, cleansing and protecting, especially against negativity.

ROSE QUARTZ ... translucent to clear pink. Possesses healing qualities for the mind. It can help with migraine and headaches. It excites the imagination, helps to release pent-up emotions, lifts spirits and dispels negative thoughts. Eases both emotional and sexual imbalances and increases fertility. Good for spleen, kidneys and circulatory system. Coupled with Hematite, works wonders on aches and pains throughout the whole body.

RUBY ... blood red. Plays a vital role in micro-surgery as a cauterising instrument. Used to alleviate all kinds of blood disorders, anaemia, poor circulation, heart disease, rheumatism and arthritis. Helps ease worries; lifts the spirits. Improves confidence, intuition and spiritual wisdom, courage and energy; produces joy, dispels fear and strengthens willpower. Gives strength in leadership and success over challengers.

RUTILATED QUARTZ ... clear Quartz which contains titanium oxide in the form of slender needles; these amplify the energy of the Quartz. It aids healing, eases bronchial problems and increases tissue growth. Also stimulates mental activity and eases depression, improves decisiveness, strength of will, and helps to communicate with the higher self.

SAPPHIRE ... related to Ruby. A range of colours, but best known and loved for the dark blue variety. Worn to stimulate the 'third eye', to expand wisdom during meditation. A sacred gem worn by kings to ward off evil. Good for improving the state of mind, increasing clarity of thought and dispelling confusion. Calms the nerves, attracts good influences and strengthens faith. Reputed to lengthen life, keeping its wearers looking young. Fortifies the heart and is a guardian of love, feelings and emotions.

SMOKEY QUARTZ ... looks exactly as its name implies - smokey. A grounding stone. Ideal around electrical goods such as computers, because it disperses negative patterns and vibrations. It can draw out and absorb negative energies, replacing them with positive. Alleviates moods, depression and other negative emotions; protects against despair, grief and anger. Used in meditation, it helps explore the inner self by penetrating dark areas with light and love. A 'Dream Stone'.

SODALITE ... deep blue with veined white flecks; often mistaken for Lapis Lazuli, but lacks the golden flecks. Calms and clears the mind, enhancing communication and insight with the higher self. A good stone for people who are over-sensitive and defensive. Brings joy and relieves a heavy heart. When placed at the side of the bed it can make a sad person wake up full of the joys of spring. Imparts youth and freshness to its wearer. When coupled with Rhodonite it produces the 'Elixir of Life'.

TIGER EYE ... generally associated with yellow to chocolate-brown. An irridescent combination of colour, resembling the gleaming eye of a tiger at night. The stone has a shifting lustre of golden light across it. Inspires brave but sensible behaviour with great insight and clearer perception. Fights hypochondria and psychosomatic diseases. A true 'confidence stone'. It attracts good luck, protects from witchcraft, and is an ideal 'worry stone' (let the stone do the worrying). Always carry one for protection.

TOPAZ ... many different colours, the most popular being rose-red to pure white. Named after the island Topazion. Known as the 'abundant one'; a stone of strength; a charm against fires and accidents. Promotes good health by overcoming stress, depression, exhaustion, fears and worries. Good for soothing, tranquillising, calming and protecting.

TOURMALINE ... has a colour for all seven of the Chakras. A master physician from the mineral world, working on all Chakra levels. A strong protector against misfortune and misunderstandings, it attracts goodwill, love and friendships. It settles troubled minds, gives confidence, inspires, calms the nerves, expands mental energy and helps clarity of thought.

TURQUOISE ... an opaque, light blue to green mineral. A sacred stone to native American Indians, and a powerful talisman to the Egyptians and the Turkish. A Lucky Stone, a protector against radiation and dark forces; a talisman favoured by horse-riders. A good all-round general healer, gentle, cooling and soothing; a stone that brings wisdom and psychic connection to the Universal Spirit. Turquoise strengthens and aligns all Chakras and energy fields. An absorber of negativity, a guardian against failure and poverty.

UNIKITE ... usually green with red patches. A variety of granite. Its name is taken from the Unaka range of mountains in North Carolina, USA. Autumnal in colour, it is a beautiful stone. It helps the wearer to relax and find peace of mind. It works mainly on a higher plain rather than the physical, going beyond into the spiritual world to find truth, bringing an understanding the true cause of disease and discomfort.

ZIRCON ... from the Arabic word 'Zarkun' ('vermilion'). Similar to Diamond in lustre and colour and often used as a substitute for diamonds. Known as the 'stone of virtue', it strengthens the mind and brings joy to the heart. Represents vitality, and works with the 'crown' Chakra, helping to connect to Universal Truth. Good for intuition, integrity, insomnia and depression.

Birthstones

On the next page you will find a list of twelve Birthstones. In my research I studied over 17 different lists. My list is the same as the Bible's list for Aries, Virgo and Pisces.

These lists have been heavily researched. There are others. However, I believe the first list to be authentic. The second list gives the most popular precious stones for the United Kingdom; and the third list is taken from the Bible: a 'New Jerusalem'.

BIRTHSTONES

Zodiac Star signs	Semi-precious Stones	Precious Stones	Bible Rev. 21-19
ARIES (21 Mar. - 20 Apr.)	Red Jasper	Diamond	Jasper
TAURUS {21 Apr. - 21 May.)	Rose Quartz	Emerald	Sapphire
GEMINI (22 May. - 21 Jun.)	Black Onyx	Pearl	Chalcedony
CANCER (22 Jun. - 22 Jul.)	Mother of Pearl	Ruby	Emerald
LEO (23 Jul. - 23 Aug.)	Tiger Eye	Peridot	Sardonyx
VIRGO (24 Aug. - 22 Sep.)	Carnelian	Sapphire	Carnelian
LIBRA (23 Sep. - 23 Oct.)	Green Aventurine	Opal	Chroysolite
SCORPIO (24 Oct. - 22 Nov.)	Rhodonite	Topaz	Beryl
SAGITTARIUS (23 Nov. - 21 Dec.)	Sodalite	Turquoise	Topaz
CAPRICORN (22 Dec. - 20 Jan.)	Obsidian Snowflake	Garnet	Chrysoprase
AQUARIUS (21 Jan. -19 Feb.)	Blue Agate	Amethyst	Jacinth
PISCES (20 Feb. - 20 Mar.)	Amethyst	Aquamarine	Amethyst

Use your Wisdom - the ability to think and act utilising knowledge, experience, understanding, common sense and insight.

According to the teachings of the Holy Quran:
The Universal Life Force, the maker and sustainer of the world, the creator of and provider for man, the Active Force and Effective Power in Nature are all one and the same, known to some as Allah and to others as God. This is the secret of all secrets and the most supreme of all beings.

Belief in God and His great power alone can provide mankind with the best possible explanation of many mysterious things in life. This is the safest way to true knowledge and spiritual insight, the right path to good behaviour and sound morals, the surest guide to happiness and prosperity.

And finally.
In this world of uncertainties you will, as you travel along your journey through life, discover that not everything goes quite according to plan. At these times in our lives it's often reassuring to realise that deep down within the very heart of our souls, we know that there's more to this life than meets the eye, and that reaching out through the mysteries of life we all have our own guides, our angels helping us through. We are part of creation, just as Gemstones and Crystals are. We are all connected to the universe; by looking beyond our world we will in time realise that the things which we seek outside, we already have within.

Gemstones and Crystals are tools to help to connect to that which we desire. It's like making a phone call to a helpline: the Gemstones and Crystals are the phone, we do the dialling and the asking, and then we hope that the Universal Life Force can help. Now dial the number that best suits you.

See your local stockist first, for any Gemstones and Crystals mentioned in this publication. If you are having difficulty obtaining any of the stones mentioned, we do offer our own mail order service and would be more than pleased to supply any of the stones listed in the form of Tumblestones. These are smooth, rounded stones ideal for use as Birthstones or as Healing Crystals.

For further details - write to:
Rosewood
P.O. Box 219, Huddersfield, West Yorkshire. HD2 2YT

E-mail enquiries to: info@rosewood-gifts.co.uk

Or why not visit our website for even more information:

www. rosewood-gifts.co.uk

Other titles in the 'POWER FOR LIFE' series:

Discover your own Special Birthstone and the renowned Healing Powers of Crystals REF. (BK1) A look at Birthstones, personality traits and characteristics associated with each Sign of the Zodiac – plus a guide to the author's own unique range of Power Gems.

A Special Glossary of Healing Stones plus Birthstones REF. (BK2) An introduction to Crystal Healing, with an invaluable Glossary listing common ailments and suggesting combinations of Gemstones/Crystals.

Create a Wish Kit using a Candle, a Crystal and the Imagination of Your Mind REF. (BK3) 'The key to happiness is having dreams; the key to success is making dreams come true.' This book will help you achieve.

Gemstone & Crystal Elixirs – Potions for Love, Health, Wealth, Energy and Success REF. (BK4) An ancient form of 'magic', invoking super-natural powers. You won't believe the power you can get from a drink!

Crystal Pendulum for Dowsing REF. (BK5) An ancient knowledge for unlocking your Psychic Power, to seek out information not easily available by any other means. Contains easy-to-follow instructions.

Crystal Healing – Fact or Fiction? Real or Imaginary? REF. (BK6) Find the answer in this book. Discover a hidden code used by Jesus Christ for healing, and read about the science of light and colour. It's really amazing.

How to Activate the Hidden Power in Gemstones and Crystals REF. (BK7) The key is to energise the thought using a crystal. The conscious can direct – but discover the real power. It's all in this book.

Astrology: The Secret Code REF. (BK8) In church it's called 'Myers Briggs typology'. In this book it's called 'psychological profiling'. If you read your horoscope, you need to read this to find your true birthstone.

Talismans, Charms and Amulets REF. (BK9) Making possible the powerful transformations which we would not normally feel empowered to do without a little extra help. Learn how to make a lucky talisman.

A Guide to the Mysteries surrounding Gemstones & Crystals REF. (BK10) Crystal healing, birthstones, crystal gazing, lucky talismans, elixirs, crystal dowsing, astrology, rune stones, amulets and rituals.

Change Your Life by Using the Most Powerful Crystal on Earth REF. (BK12) The most powerful crystal on earth can be yours. A book so disarmingly simple to understand, yet with a tremendous depth of knowledge.

All the above books are available from your local stockist,
or, if not, from the publisher.

NOTES

Welcome to the world of Rosewood

An extract from a 'thank- you' letter for one of my books.

"I realised just how much you really had indeed understood me and my need for direction and truly have allowed me the confidence and strength to know and believe I can achieve whatever I want in life"

If you like natural products, hand-crafted gifts including Gemstone jewellery, objects of natural beauty – the finest examples from Mother Nature, tinged with an air of Mystery – then we will not disappoint you.
For those who can enjoy that feeling of connection with the esoteric nature of Gemstones and Crystals, then our 'Power for Life – Power Bracelets could be ideal for you.
Each bracelet comes with its own guide explaining a way of thinking that's so powerful it will change your life and the information comes straight from the Bible.
e.g. read Mark 11: 22

We regularly give inspirational talks on
Crystal Power – fact or fiction?
A captivating story about the world's fascination with natural gemstones and crystals and how the Placebo effect explains the healing power of gemstones and crystals – it's intriguing.
And it's available on a CD

To see our full range of books, jewellery and gifts including CD's and DVD'S

Visit our web site - www.rosewood-gifts.co.uk

To see our latest videos go to 'You Tube'
and type in Rosewood Gifts.